THE HAND OF MAN ON AMERICA

David Plowden # THE HAND OF MAN ON AMERICA

THE CHATHAM PRESS, INC.   RIVERSIDE, CONNECTICUT

International Standard Book Number: 0-85699-077-9
Library of Congress Catalog Card Number: 74-127823
Printed in the United States of America by Eastern Press, Inc.

FOR PLEASANCE

PREFACE

The photographs of this book reflect my grave concern over what is happening to America today. Originally I photographed because I felt love and admiration for what I saw and I wanted to document some of our magnificent creations, such as our heroic machines and the great though often anonymous examples of our building art, many of which are disappearing. As I photographed, however, almost imperceptibly I became aware that in focusing on past achievements alone I was not portraying the America which in fact we now are living in. I felt an urgent necessity to photograph the country as it was being transformed and our increasingly dismal condition which we seem to accept so easily. For the time being, therefore, I put aside the documentation of other generations in order to record the America of my own time.

As a photographer I have turned to the way I know best to express my deep distress over our appalling indifference and our misplaced priorities. I have tried to show on the one hand what we are capable of and on the other what we are doing.

I can only hope that my pictures will in some way help us to see elements in our surroundings that we have up to now ignored, and in seeing them, we may react to them.

These photographs were not taken specifically with this book in mind, but rather they have been slowly gathered during many trips into the land with my wife, Pleasance, in the last ten years. They were brought to the attention of Eugene Ostroff, Curator of Photography at the Smithsonian Institution, who arranged for them to be exhibited there and subsequently to be offered by the Smithsonian's Traveling Exhibition Service. It was his idea that the show be titled, "The Hand of Man On America." I will always be indebted to him for giving me this marvelous opportunity to express myself and for the honor of having my pictures shown in this manner.

It was while they were in Mr. Ostroff's hands that the photographs were shown to the director of the Smithsonian Institution Press and the concept of a book on the same theme germinated. All books are a collaborative venture, in spite of the fact that the author is usually given full credit, and I believe that this is grossly unfair, for anyone who knows how books are made is aware that it is, in a sense, the same kind of production as for the stage; it is shaped by many people, each of whom has added to it his particular skill, knowledge, or perception. Certainly in my case it would have been totally impossible to produce this book without the enthusiasm, the interest, and all the time expended by the staff of the Smithsonian Institution Press. I would especially like to thank Stephen Kraft, whose design of its pages so fully and yet—with a gift rare among designers—unobtrusively realized my intent; and Jane Sieverts, my editor, whose sympathetic grasp of the total concept combined with attention to minute detail never impaired the original style. It was Anders Richter, former Director of the Press, who saw in the great quantity of photographs the book's ultimate structure and impressed upon me the importance of expressing my thoughts in words as well as images. Gordon Hubel, who succeeded Mr. Richter, has supported the work and brought it to a successful completion.

I would like to mention four of my friends whose opinions I deeply respect, and with whom I discussed many times the ideas which I have tried to touch upon in this book: David McCullough, author and a former conservation editor of American Heritage Magazine; Robert Vogel, Curator of Civil and Mechanical Engineering at the Smithsonian Institution, who originally put me in contact with Gene Ostroff, and whose interest in this and so many other projects has been of such great encouragement to me; Dr. William Vanderkloot, Professor and Chairman of the Department of Physiology and Biophysics of the New York University School of Medicine; and my brother-in-law, Dr. Gordon B. Younce, Department of Geology, Rutgers University, Camden, New Jersey, who has always given so much encouragement to me as a person and as a photographer.

Above everyone else, however, there is no other person to whom I owe more than to Pleasance, my wife, although I will never be able to thank her properly with words.

From the very beginning she and I have collaborated on this book and shaped it together. Without her ideas and criticism, without all the hours she spent working with me, quite apart from those she spent typing, it would never have existed.

In every sense this is Pleasance's book too.

DAVID PLOWDEN

Sea Cliff, New York March, 1971

CONTENTS

SPACE

"It is for the benefit of mankind," said Walt Whitman, that the Nation's "power and territory should be extended—the farther the better."

In our rush to fulfill what we felt was our Manifest Destiny, "to overspread and to possess the whole Continent" which we believed had been "allotted by Providence" to us, the Great Plains were the obstacle, the place which we must cross before we could explore and exploit our farthest reaches. To the endless procession of pioneers streaming westward over the rutted trails toward the Promised Land, Oregon, or the Valley of the Great Salt Lake, or to the Forty-Niner, infected with gold fever, the Plains were indeed the Great American Desert, the wilderness through which they must endure. It was an unspeakably hostile country, fraught with danger. Aside from the ever-present threat of an Indian attack, the land itself was totally alien to the white man and beyond the comprehension of either the farmer from cozy little New England or the immigrant fresh from Europe. It was unlike anything in the previous experience of those audacious enough to try to cross it.

It was a land of appalling extremes; an immoderate land, where the unprepared, and sometimes even the well-prepared, could perish. It was dry; an empty, wild country, where there was not the slightest sign of civilization beyond the wagon tracks. The scale was overwhelming, vaster than any other place on the Continent; it was a great sea of grass, where the land rose and fell almost imperceptibly in long swells, and overhead there was the sky. Said Willa Cather, "Elsewhere the sky is the roof of the world; but here the earth was the floor of the sky."

It gives a feeling of being more in space than on land, because the sky and the light, always bright, are made more bright because there is no shade. There is nothing between you and the elements, with everything exposed to the sun and the ceaseless winds. On the Plains you are in the elements, you can see forever.

The pioneers saw *more*, always more. Interminable, the same horizon was always there, never getting nearer, day after day after day, week after week, until finally there was a fragile blue line, faint above windswept yellow grasses: the Landfall of the Rockies. Thin and distant for still more days, it slowly became more clear, until at last they wound their way up into the mountain passes.

After the pioneers came the railroads, hurrying to get across the Plains, too. The eyes of their builders were set far away on the treasures of the Orient, or the minerals still locked up in the mountains, or the timber still standing in the virgin forests of the Northwest. Straight across the Plains the rails were laid, deviating neither to the left nor right from their goal. No cities yet to divert their course, no towns for them to serve, their only business along the way, cattle, was driven up the trails which came to meet the rails.

To most of us who drive "Out West," the Plains still are something to get across as quickly as possible, they are still to us the Great American Desert. We don't seem able to realize, when we are on them, that the Plains *are* the West, that we are there, in the same West we know so well when at home in front of the TV. It is the West with which we have been so preoccupied, the last frontier, the land of the Indians and the cowboys, and the buffalo, the cattle drive, Jessie James and Matt Dillon; the land from which so many of our legends and so much of our lore has sprung.

Its limitless expanse of flatness appears only a speedway over which the vacationer can race. He too, like the railroad builder, has his eyes and mind set on some distant place, somewhere else, on Yellowstone, or Yosemite, or the Pacific perhaps; never, it seems, on where he is, certainly not the "spacious skies," the amber waves of wheat all around him. The Plains are to him just mileage, measured in terms of the gas, the boring hours, it takes to cross them. The way is paved for him; the only challenge which the motorist faces is that of staying awake, his only danger, a blowout at eighty miles an hour.

But people are not the only things crossing the Plains. Even when we are not there, our lines of communication are. Today the Plains are laced with wires carrying our messages, our intimacies, our thoughts, to our brethren on the opposite coast who may never have seen the land over which their voices travel.

There are other wires too, those of the Rural Electrification projects and, more menacing, the high tension lines, traveling over the land, taking possession of it, yet giving nothing in return, so that someone else in another place may have the benefits of electricity. The Plains may give the illusion of unconquerable space, of being still the frontier; but even in the empty land, hundreds of miles from the nearest town or human being, on the horizon there are the lines; wires, roads, rails, all leading beyond to some distant place where a body of men dwell. Although these things are only the fingers, they are proof enough, however, that man holds the land in his hand, and that within his grasp is the power to change the face of it.

1   *Great Northern Railroad freight train west of Havre, Montana.*

2   *Along Route U.S. 2 in the Plains
    east of Malta, Montana.*

3   *The Great Plains near Chinook, Montana.*

On the Western Plains the ever-present horizon gives an illusion that we are on the Frontier, that over the hill there is the promise of a new world after we use this one up, a chance to start again if we fail. Beyond the horizon is the future, the unexplored territory into which our increasing millions and our baggage can pour forever. With infinite space, infinite possibilities, we needn't worry, or be careful with what we have—and so we haven't been.

4 *Approaching the ninety-eighth meridian, westbound, on highway No. 7 in Steele County, North Dakota.*

There are few places on earth which compare in fertility to the Prairie. Like the Great Plains, it is a vast treeless expanse, originally a grassland from horizon to horizon. Most of us lump the Prairie and Plains together and refer to both as the Middle West, perhaps not appreciating the tremendous difference between the two regions. The Prairie is moist; it has an average annual rainfall of twenty to forty inches. This, in combination with its beautiful soil, has made it the most productive region in America. It stretches all the way from western Ohio to the Great Plains, filling most of Indiana, Illinois, Iowa, and parts of Wisconsin and Minnesota; it pushes up into Saskatchewan and Manitoba, west into the Dakotas, and down through eastern Nebraska, Kansas, Oklahoma, and on through Texas to the Rio Grande.

Beyond the Prairie, on the other side of the ninety-eighth meridian, you are in the West, on the Plains which roll on all the way to the Rockies. Here the rainfall is only a scant ten to twenty inches a year, totally unsuited to the agriculture of the Prairie.

But the difference is more than climatic; the whole aura of the Prairie is different as well. Unlike the dry undulating grasslands of the Plains, it is nearly level; the farms seem always to be in the distance, separated from us by the ploughed earth, or fields of corn, looking like scale models, so vast is the flatness. You are aware of the earth itself, sometimes black, sometimes red, sometimes brown, but always rich and pungent and fecund. It is the American Heartland.

5 *Sunrise on the Prairie near Funks Grove, Illinois.*

6 *Prairie farm near Funks Grove, Illinois.*

7 *The skyline of lower Manhattan, from across
   the Hudson on Caven Point in Jersey City.*

THE LAND POSSESSED

And God said, let us make man in our image, after
our likeness: and let them have dominion over the
fish of the sea, and over the fowl of the air, and over
the cattle, and over all the earth.
And God blessed them, and God said unto them,
Be fruitful, and multiply, and replenish the earth,
and subdue it.
. . . and it was so.

GENESIS (1:26,28,30)

"What was it the Engines said
Pilots touching—head to head
Facing on the single track,
Half a world behind each back?"

What The Engines Said.   BRET HARTE

On May 10, 1869 at Promontory Summit,
Utah, in the midst of one of the most desolate
places imaginable, we drove the Golden
Spike. That last spike completed our first
transcontinental railroad. And the door was
closed on the Frontier.

8 *On December 25, 1830, "The Best Friend of Charleston" became the first locomotive to pull a train of cars in North America. Canadian Pacific Railway Engine Number 5145 one of the last driven by steam, was retired from service in the spring of 1960.*

Possibly the first act of possession, of staking a claim, is to fence the land. To say, "This is mine," to define one's territory, is perhaps a fundamental part of human nature; certainly, in America, fences are an integral part of the landscape.

A fence can stand for something quite beautiful, for intent to use and cherish the enclosed earth; it can also stand for Right of Possession, for the power to do what you want to with what you've got, and to exclude.

9 *Farmland near St. Fabien, Quebec, in Rimouski County in the St. Lawrence River Valley.*

"All men have a natural right to a portion of the soil; and . . ., as the use of the soil is indispensable to life, the right of all men to the soil is as sacred as their right to life itself."

"The public lands of the United States belong to the people, and should not be sold to individuals nor granted to corporations, but should be held as a sacred trust for the benefit of the people, and should be granted in limited quantities, free of cost to land-less settlers."

These two statements, incorporated in the platform of the Free Soil Party during the Campaign of 1854, are the essence of the free land movement, advocated for so many years by the western settlers and culminating in the Homestead Act signed into law by President Lincoln on May 20, 1862.

By this law, "any person who is head of a family, or who has arrived at the age of twenty-one years, and is a citizen of the United States, or who shall have filed his declaration of intention to become such" could acquire a quarter-section, 160 acres, of unoccupied public land, free of charge save for the nominal filing fee of $10, by living on it for five years and improving it.

Although the demand for free land increased as the West became settled, for many years this movement did not have enough Congressional influence to bring about the passage of a Homestead law. The opposition against it was very strong indeed. The South naturally opposed anything which might cause the territories to be peopled by anti-slave forces, and the East felt it would create a mass exodus, thus adversely affecting its dominant economic situation, and deflating its land values. But the strongest opposition was from the Federal Government itself, which obtained a substantial revenue from the sale of public domain. It wasn't until after the southern states had seceded and Lincoln had become President that his Republican Party was able to fulfill its campaign promise to secure passage of Homestead legislation.

Although the Act was a great blessing to many a man who was willing to work a farm and had not the cash to pay for the land, and even though it undeniably did much to encourage the settlement of our empty spaces, many of the half-a-million families who took advantage of it were bitterly disillusioned. One hundred and sixty acres of dry range were not comparable to one hundred and sixty acres of rich, wet, Eastern land. Many farmers found themselves unable to produce enough for subsistence on the acreage given them. A verse from a ballad of the time tells the story:

> Hurrah for Greer County! The land of
> the free,
> The land of the bedbug, grasshopper, and
> flea;
> I'll sing of its praises, I'll tell of its fame,
> While starving to death on my government
> claim.

Unfortunately, the Act provided a bonanza for the speculator and land grabber, and the country was probably defrauded out of more public domain than the legitimate farmer ever made use of. Yet the idea of giving land away to someone who will work it is a compelling one. It was more than just a means of settling our country.

Most of the land settled under the Homestead Act was on the Great Plains west of the Mississippi but the word itself, homestead, means any house, most particularly a farmhouse, no matter where it is. The concept of homestead stands for our right to possess a piece of land, which is a basic tenet of the American philosophy.

10 *Homestead near Piqua, Ohio.*

There is always a question about what architecture really is, of how to distinguish between Architecture and Building as John Ruskin insisted we must. According to him, "Architecture concerns itself only with those characters of an edifice which are above and beyond its common use." Furthermore, he stated that architecture must be confined to "certain characters venerable or beautiful, but otherwise unnecessary." There is no question that many utilitarian buildings cannot qualify as architecture, but this is the result of bad design, not of their function. Ruskin's definition seems to exclude many industrial buildings, whose design, while primarily concerned with nothing beyond the structure's "common use," still creates very powerful forms with an "unintentional" beauty of their own. The grain elevator is but one domestic example, which has been appreciated by many renowned architects.

H. H. Richardson, for instance, nearly a century ago was said to have remarked that one of the things he would most like to design was a grain elevator. At that time, however, he was an exception, for most nineteenth-century American architects, unlike today's engineers, seemed so concerned with creation of facades in the style of various revivals that, as a professional group, they were perhaps oblivious to a real American architecture evolving in another area altogether. Europeans recognized it before most of us. Certainly Walter Gropius, organizer of the famed "Bauhaus," did when he said: "The grain elevators, . . . the coal conveyors of the great railway lines, and the more modern industrial plants of North America are almost as impressive in their monumental power as the buildings of ancient Egypt. They present an architectural composition of such exactness that to the observer their meaning is forcefully and unequivocally clear." But perhaps the best case in defense of these forms lies in a statement by the great Le Corbusier:

"Architecture is the masterly, correct and magnificent play of masses brought together in light. Our eyes are made to see forms in light; light and shade reveal these forms; cubes, cones, spheres, cylinders or pyramids are the great primary forms which light reveals to advantage; the image of these is distinct and tangible within us and without ambiguity. It is for that reason that these are beautiful forms, the most beautiful forms. Everybody is agreed as to that, the child, the savage, and the metaphysician. It is of the very nature of the plastic arts. . . . The architects of today, lost in the sterile backwaters of their plans, their foliage, their pilasters and their lead roofs, have never acquired the conception of primary masses. They were never taught that at the schools. Not in the pursuit of an architectural idea, but simply guided by the results of calculation (derived from the principles which govern our universe) and the conception of A LIVING ORGANISM, the ENGINEERS of to-day make use of the primary elements and, by co-ordinating them in accordance with the rules, provoke in us architectural emotions and thus make the work of man ring in unison and universal order.

Thus we have the American grain elevators and factories, the magnificent FIRST-FRUITS of the new age. THE AMERICAN ENGINEERS OVERWHELM WITH THEIR CALCULATIONS OUR EXPIRING ARCHITECTURE."

Perhaps the grain elevator can be called the indigenous architecture of the Plains and the Prairie, where it has created a regional form of freestanding skyscraper.

11   *Grain elevator, North Topeka, Kansas.*

To the Head-of-the-Lakes, at Duluth and Superior, have trundled an endless number of the world's heaviest freight trains, carrying the commerce of the continent: Dakota, Montana, and Minnesota grain, and iron ore from the Mesabi and the other ranges in the hinterlands. Out of these great deposits were scooped eighty-five percent of the ore used in our iron and steel mills, before we exhausted the supply in fighting two World Wars. For years it was the greatest port on the Lakes. So great was its annual tonnage that it was second only to New York harbor in the entire country, a rank which is even more astounding when one considers the fact that the Lakes are closed to navigation during the winter months. Today, though Head-of-the-Lakes no longer moves the volume that it once did, the Bunyanesque machinery of the harbor is still there. Its gigantic forms, the ore docks and grain elevators, completely overwhelm the boats which draw up beside them to fill their holds.

12   *Grain elevator, Toulon, Kansas.*

13   *Grain elevator, Superior, Wisconsin.*

Our Great Lakes System is the largest body
of fresh water on the Earth. Reaching half-
way across the Continent, it provides us
with the most superb of all inland waterways over which millions upon millions of
tons of commerce—wheat, coal, iron ore—
glide each year.

Since before the turn of the century, most
of this cargo has been carried in the holds of
that vessel indigenous to the Lakes, the bulk
carrier, known familiarly as the "Laker."
As many of these are still steam-driven,
they make up what is probably the largest
fleet of steamboats in the world today and,
in fact, are the last major use of steam pro-
pulsion in the world of transportation.

Most of the boats are old, forty or fifty
years old, which is very old indeed for a piece
of machinery. Their longevity is due in
part to the fact that fresh water is kinder to
metal than salt water.

14　s/s Algosoo, *built in 1907 for the Algoma Central &*
Hudson Bay Railway to haul wheat down from the
Head-of-the-Lakes. The pronounced overhang
of her counterstern made the ship more maneuverable
in tight quarters without decreasing her deck space.

Wherever you look in America there is a
wire, as if spun by some giant spider,
with the land his victim.

15   *One hundred and eighty-five miles north of Los Angeles in California's Owens Valley.*

Chicago is the Railroad Capital of the world; upon it converge more railroads than on any other city in America.

Through its freight yards more than 34,000 cars pass each day, twelve million cars a year. Which means, statistically speaking, that every freight car in the Nation passes through Chicago nearly once a month.

16 *Railroad yards on the South Side of Chicago, Illinois.*

When man first placed the steam engine in the hold of a vessel and ran it successfully in 1807, he brought about a revolution on the waters equivalent only to that which the locomotive was to bring about on the land two decades later.

Now mankind possessed a device which freed him from the unpredictability of the natural forces upon which he had depended. With this machine, we could for the first time utilize our magnificent system of natural waterways. The machine was powerful enough to battle upstream against the currents of the Mississippi, heretofore a downstream-only channel of commerce. We were able at last to exploit the hitherto inaccessible realm of the Great Lakes, where before we had always been at the mercy of the winds.

Although the age of steam is over, its importance in our development is not diminished by the fact that, from our vantage point deep in another era, we are largely unaware of it.

Some species of boats, such as the great passenger boats and the river packets, have become extinct with the end of "steamboating"; not because they were steam-driven, but because, as a class, their functions were more economically performed by other means of transport. That ubiquitous little creature the tug, however, remains one of the most familiar of all boats, and is still found in nearly every port. The great fleets of steam tugs are gone, however. One of the last belonged to the New York Central Railroad and operated in New York Harbor until it was retired early in 1968 when the railroad became part of the merged Penn-Central.

17 *New York Central No. 31, one of the last active steam tugs in North America, on the Hudson River in New York Harbor, shortly before her retirement in 1968.*

Bridges, strictly speaking, are not architecture. Unfortunately, however, we have sometimes tried to design them so as to de-emphasize the steelwork, whose nakedness seems to offend us. By dressing them up with superfluous adornment we must feel somehow that we have made bridges more acceptable. This has often been true of bridges at particularly prominent crossings, where we are apt to overstate their intrinsic monumentality.

During the period of "social architecture" in the late Twenties and the Thirties this practice was particularly rife, and the results often more intimidating than ingratiating.

18 *The pylons guarding the portal of the Yaquina Bay Bridge, built in 1936 at Newport, Oregon, seem a more appropriate setting for Mussolini's Black Shirts than for tourists sightseeing on Oregon's Coast.*

20 *The absolutely indestructible-looking Point Bridge across the Monongahela River at Pittsburgh's Golden Triangle is doomed.*
A few hundred yards upstream the brand-new Fort Pitt Bridge, built as part of the city's downtown redevelopment scheme which created a park at the point, carries the traffic from the Triangle.
The Point Bridge, built in 1927, is not, however, the first on the site. Pittsburgh, which of all American cities can be truly called the "bridge city," for years has been building and rebuilding its multitude of crossings, and in the course of its history probably experimented with the greatest variety of bridges on the American continent. The first bridge at the point, built in 1876, was a unique form of eye-bar suspension bridge and was an even more extraordinary example of the bridge builders' art than the presently abandoned one which, in fact, is an extremely interesting form of cantilever construction.
Its replacement is, unfortunately, a rather mundane-looking arch, more the product of the computer than of an individual bridge builder's genius.

19 *The fantastic roller-coaster undulations of one of the San Francisco area's most spectacular bridges, the Richmond-San Rafael Bridge across the entrance to San Pablo Bay, are the result of pure economics. The two ship channels necessitated high-level spans, but in-between and on either side the roadway dips in order to save steel in the piers.*

Roads don't destroy natural beauty, they take people to it and in some cases even create it.

THE ENGINEERING NEWS-RECORD

Ladies and Gentlemen, if beauty is in the eyes of the beholder, where is it if people cannot go and see it? If our generation and succeeding ones become—as seems likely— more and more conscious of beauty, it will be because every road that is built can and should make more and more beauty accessible to more people. In a year's time, a few hundred people may be able to afford the time and energy to *hike* through a woods or park. But every day hundreds of *thousands* may *drive* through these woods and parks, when carefully designed highways unfurl the whole lovely view.

H. E. HUMPHREYS,
U.S. Rubber Company

I am for better roads. We need more of them. I am the chairman of the Subcommittee on Roads in the Public Works Committee. We want more roads.

JOHN C. KLUCZYNSKI,
Congressman from Illinois

21   *The North-East Freeway, Interstate 85, near Atlanta, Georgia.*

22   *Geronimo, Oklahoma, is on the little-used tracks of a Rock Island Line branch which serves nearby Fort Sill. It is here that the notorious Apache chieftain was imprisoned after his final surrender in 1886, and near where he later settled down to farm away the years until his death in 1909.*

HABITAT

Habitat is by definition: 1. The area or type of environment in which an organism or biological population lives or occurs. 2. The place where a person or thing is most likely to be found.

Our habitat is basically self-made but, tragically, we are destroying it as we destroy most things we touch. Perhaps we are not meant to survive as a species, for certainly we are making our environment less and less livable. We are polluting the landscape as well as the air and water, not just with the effluence of society and its technology, but with architectural sewage as well.

Most of us, I believe, ignore our habitat because of its familiarity and because the routine of life occupies our attention so completely. We don't *look*, at either the bad *or* the good, because we don't consider the elements special; they haven't been pointed out to us, they are not something we go to see. Not being concerned with our surroundings, we are apt to overlook the fact that the familiar, indigenous architecture of our neighborhoods and main streets often presents a surprising variety of forms and styles frequently both beautiful and ingenious. Though most would not be considered national or historic monuments in the usual sense of the phrase, some of the finest examples of our building art can be found in this anonymous architecture. They are usually not the creations of the great architects, nor always the products of formal architectural training, but of the resourcefulness of the American people whose native genius has frequently been expressed in the individuality of

their building. Often these structures are far more representative of America than are the Mount Vernons or reconstructed Williamsburgs. Sadly, however, we usually tear down, mutilate, or let these beautiful buildings deteriorate beyond repair before we realize their value.

In contrast with the ingenuity of which Americans have proven themselves so capable in the past, the engineering and building art of today seems almost devoid of inspiration and individuality. With a very few exceptions, contemporary construction presents an abysmal appearance and outlook for the future. One finds it hard to believe that the *human being* has been considered in these designs. The slip-shod, mass-produced, get-it-up-and-paid-for-as-quickly-as-possible look is everywhere, along with the neat, antiseptic, secure, totally uninteresting and deadening architecture of the suburbs. But just as we usually don't look at the good in our habitat, somehow we don't seem to notice the horror which threatens to engulf us. This horror is the very dullness and mundaneness which we are creating and which cannot help but deaden the spirit—and, in the end, our very ability to react to it.

Or, perhaps, it does not occur to most people that they *can* object. It seems that most of us would prefer to remain a part of the "Silent Majority," which apparently does not see a need for change. I believe that our general acquiescence to this mediocrity is a symptom of a much graver condition: a basic indifference to our whole environment.

The expressway can take no form but ugliness. A high-speed passage beneath Brooklyn Heights serves to preserve the neighborhood and even to enhance it with an esplanade above the roadways, but the character of the urban freeway itself is unalterable.

24   *Brooklyn Queens Expressway, connecting the two boroughs.*

Seventy-five years ago the scene presented by the north side of Main Street in Cazenovia, New York, would have been commonplace.

At first glance it seems indistinguishable from any one of a thousand American main streets; but look again—the building facades are totally unspoiled, unchanged, and in their original condition from sidewalk to roofline.

In almost every town, while the upper stories of the buildings may remain unchanged, the store fronts below have almost universally undergone some sort of transformation, usually with the most unfortunate aesthetic and architectural consequences. Sadly, most merchants have been persuaded that if they present "up-to-date," progressive-looking facades, their images will be enhanced and their businesses will prosper, with the result that most of these storefronts are not only ugly but stereotyped because of a dearth of imagination in the building trade. Most of these formerly distinctive streets have become a jumbled mess of conflicting signs and incongruous shapes behind which the buildings hide. One need only to look at Cazenovia or a few other notable communities, such as Galena, Illinois, or Nantucket, Massachusetts, to see the opportunities. Cazenovia's street is not only very beautiful, but is unique in that it is a functioning main street, whose occupants were well aware of its value and took pains to preserve it, and in that the original character of the organic street has been maintained. Elsewhere a single preserved building is often totally lost in its incongruous surroundings.

The importance of this particular endeavor is that it is solely the work of the people of the community, not of a foundation or an agency of government.

It is not a restoration, nor a museum, both of which are inevitably filled with quaintnesses and inauthentic periodizations, such as gas lamps and costumed artisans plying defunct trades for the benefit of tourists. It seems that the moment we decide to save a site we must endow it with some significance to make it "historic" and so that it can be a touristic success; but by merely restoring it, we embalm it, we remove its soul, it is dead.

25 In 1966 this side of Cazenovia's Main Street was selected by the New York State Council on Arts to be a recipient of the New York State Award.

The motorist who speeds over the highway with undeterred determination to reach his destination, be it a campground, a sales meeting, or Sunday lunch with Mother, rarely if ever thinks of the towns he encounters as anything more than an irritant, something to slow him up. The highway engineers, catering to him, usually have by-passed each town by a mile or so. From the highway these little communities are nothing more than an intersection, the town no more than its name on a sign pointing to it. Invariably it is flanked by a service station or two, whose familiar trade marks have conditioned the motorist to buy from Texaco, Phillips, or Gulf, not from a Mr. Stewart, who is totally unknown to him.

But if perchance he does happen to go into town, no doubt there would be, in some fairly prominent location, probably near the end of the street, an establishment like Stewart's Garage, known by the name of the individual who owns it, rather than by the name of the gasoline he sells.

26   *Dr. M. H. Porter's office in the old bank building on the corner of Main and First Streets, Parkston, South Dakota.*

27   *Stewart's Garage, Cement, Oklahoma.*

28 *Sidewalk clock in front of florist on the Main Street of Beacon, New York.*

29   *Main Street, Apache, Oklahoma, where there are still many of Geronimo's descendants among the shoppers.*

30   *A bank which failed in the Dust Bowl. Corner of Main Street, Apache, Oklahoma.*

31
The Pink Elephant Saloon,
Fredericksburg, Texas.

There have always been traditional places of common congregation for simple talk. These have been the general store or the post office (which were often one and the same), the railroad station, or the ferry house; places where it was warm, where paths crossed, where people waited.

The railroad station and ferry house are gone, general stores are scarce, and the new post offices are hardly conducive to relaxed talk. The only public place like them left today seems to be the laundromat. People *have* to stop, to wait, and so they talk, while their clothes bump ceaselessly in the machines.

32 *The laundromat in Gotebo,
Oklahoma, is one of the few
places open in this virtually
abandoned town.*

33 *Unused Congregational Church*
in Williamsville, Vermont.

34 *Roman Catholic Church at Inkerman,*
New Brunswick, population under 500,
far out on a peat-producing peninsula
in the Gulf of St. Lawrence.

35 *First Assembly of God,
Lawton, Oklahoma.*

36 *Side of movie theater, Paramus, New Jersey.*

The familiar roadside diner derives its name and shape from another type of diner, almost unknown to the majority of travelers today, the railroad dining car. It was once considered an indispensable part of any decent passenger train; in an era when you went by rail if you wanted to get across the land, a meal in such a diner was an occasion.

Although the word, diner, has come to mean almost any place where one can stop for a cup of coffee, a true diner of the highway bears a vestigial resemblance to its wheeled prototype in its same general appearance: long and low, with an unbroken row of windows. More often than not, however, this is just facade, a veneer of aluminum or some other flashy material pasted up on one side only.

Most of us come to a diner through necessity, to eat as quickly as possible and be on our way again. The incessant clattering of heavy Shenango ware, the smell of bad grease frying, the formica counters, do not calm. The diner, then, has come to represent "anti-dining," it is not a place to linger and it does not cater to lingering. Like the other "Food" and "Fuel" stops, it provides only the bare necessities to the hurrying traveler. The human soul and spirit have been overlooked, forgotten in our hurry to hurry.

37 *Rear view of diner, seen from the railroad station in Whitehall, New York.*

38   *Rear view of diner, Route U.S. 22, in New Jersey.*

Phoebe Snow was the mythical young lady who made the Lackawanna railroad famous around the turn of the century. All dressed in white, she always descended smilingly from the train at the journey's end. She was celebrated in jingles advertising the fact that, unlike those of other railroads, the Lackawanna locomotives burned the same clean hard coal which was the bread and butter of the railroad's freight business.

In the days before air-conditioning, when the only way to cool down the cars was to ride with the windows open, travelers frequently arrived at their destinations spattered by the soot which had rained down upon them from the clouds of soft coal smoke from the locomotive. However, before you planned your next trip to Scranton or down the line to Buffalo, you might remember that:

"Miss Snow alights, her frock still white
She took the road of anthracite."

Many years later, the Lackawanna revived Phoebe Snow by naming its brandnew, air-conditioned, and diesel-powered train between Hoboken and Buffalo after her.

Phoebe Snow, the train, didn't survive for long and the Lackawanna is now the silent partner of the newly merged Erie–Lackawanna system, which today is merely a subsidiary of a still larger corporation.

39 *The Phoebe Snow, shortly before she was discontinued, under the Bush trainshed at Scranton, Pennsylvania. This magnificent station was the result of a competition held in 1907, won by the architect Kenneth Murchison.*

40 *Commuter cars parked in front of the Erie-Lackawanna depot at Tenafly, New Jersey, once the home of financier Hetty Green, called the richest woman in America at the turn of the century.*

Much of nineteenth-century architecture has been criticized for its concern with appearance, with the adornments and ornaments of buildings and the stress on decorative values at the expense of structural ones, and, though it is true that until nearly the close of the century we cared more for molding the surfaces than emphasizing functional problems, which were left to engineers or carpenters to solve, our motive was to make buildings pleasing both inside and out. In spite of their preoccupation with creating a good impression rather than a good structure, nineteenth-century architects were at least far more concerned with how we looked, and how where we lived looked, than we are now. If today we sometimes create better architecture *per se*, we certainly haven't produced a better habitat in which to live.

In the early part of the nineteenth century we had not yet developed structural iron and steel, the materials through which we would discover our very own architecture. As a child looks to its mother for guidance, we looked to European civilizations for our initial inspirations. In the process we borrowed from older styles and orders which were long established, and these adaptations came to be known as revivals. By the late 1830s the Gothic Revival was replacing the Greek in vogue. As Victorians, we quite possibly felt that the Grecian forms were immoral, un-Christian, and that a "heathen temple" was hardly an appropriate form for a dwelling. In any case, we spurned the pure classical form for the more romantic and picturesque vein of the Gothic Revival, which ushered in the Victorian period of architecture in America.

One of the most influential spokesmen for this revival was Andrew Jackson Downing, the noted landscape architect who, through the influence of his prolific writing, was credited with having "made over the face of rural America." Though Downing's concern may have been more with creating beautiful "surroundings" than with architecture itself, this did not diminish his effect on building. He was disturbed not merely by the "tasteless Temples" which he thought were proliferating in our countryside, but he was also one of the few Americans to voice genuine concern about the way most of us lived, and about the effect of our environment on us. "So long as men are forced to dwell in log huts and follow the hunter's life," he wrote, "we must not be surprised at the lynch law and the use of the bowie knife. But when smiling lawns and tasteful cottages begin to embellish a country, we know that order and culture are established."

Downing's writings, with the drawings of the contemporary architect Alexander Jackson Davis, were the prototype for the so-called pattern books from which so many examples of "carpenter Gothic" sprang forth. This was an era of relatively few trained architects and designers in America (the first architectural school wasn't founded until mid-century), but of many ingenious people who, by necessity, had learned enough of the various building trades to live in a world where specialization had not yet spread out into society. Those who wanted to erect a dwelling or a public building and wanted it to be "artistic" or "a noble specimen of architecture," which meant it had to be in style, often turned to these pattern books for their guidance. In matters of taste, then as now, we Americans have always been unsure of ourselves, dependent on texts and prescriptions.

These pattern books were not limited to "Gothic Cottages," for within their pages were to be found a whole spectrum of dwellings, with such choice items as "Tuscan" and "Pompeian Suburban Villas" or "Lancastrian Embattled Mansions." With a sense of Victorian propriety, they also provided numerous plans for lesser dwellings which the tastemakers deemed appropriate for the lower classes, designs for "A Cottage for a Mechanic or a Clerk," for example.

Whether today we consider these things bogus monstrosities or fantastic examples of architectural inventiveness is a matter of choice, and irrelevant besides, for what is important is that we were obviously more concerned then with the appearance of even mass-produced things. The mass-produced clerk's bungalow of today is a characterless example of developer's architecture, if, in fact, it can be called architecture at all.

41
The design for this rather subdued example of "Carpenter Gothic" in Macedon, New York, was probably taken from the pages of a "pattern book."

Architecture has been classified into nearly as many styles as there are species of birds, and just as it is possible to enjoy a bird's song without further knowledge, so a building can be appreciated without being categorized.

The question of whether this typical turn-of-the-century house in New York State is the highly improbable style known as "Queen Anne," which had absolutely no connection with the ruler of the same name whatsoever, or whether it is some other illegitimate style—is immaterial. For the house is a perfect example of pleasant residential street architecture often unnoticed because it is familiar to us all.

42 *Newark, New York.*

Architecture is the art which so disposes and adorns the edifices raised by man for whatsoever uses, that the sight of them may contribute to his mental health, power and pleasure.

JOHN RUSKIN,
The Seven Lamps of Architecture

43   *A home near Troy Hills, New Jersey.*

44   *Row houses in Covington, Kentucky.*

45   *Batten and board barn in the town of Guilford, Vermont.*

The Monongahela River flows northward to Pittsburgh, where it joins the Allegheny to form the Ohio River. Its valley is deep and narrow and agonizingly twisted and is fantastically choked with stacks and smoke and the mysterious shapes of the great iron and steel mills. An unbroken chain of monotonously bleak towns differing only in their names clings to both river banks and clambers up the steep hillsides as if to escape the turmoil below.

From a distant vantage point the view of the industrial spectacle below can be as breathtaking a sight as the Grand Canyon. But from street level, the view is unspeakably depressing, the air foul, the streets sordid, the architecture bad, the houses unpainted. The valley is filled with tales of human suffering and conflict.

In 1892 the city of Homestead, not far upriver from Pittsburgh, was the site of one of the bitterest labor disputes in our country's history: The Homestead Strike. Before it was brutally broken by Frick and his "Pinkertons," blood ran in the streets.

Further up the valley, at Donora, 5,000 people succumbed and over twenty died in 1948 from the "Donora Smog" which lay in the valley for days on end.

Not far downstream from Donora, at Clairton, on the bank opposite the huge and seductively photographic coke works, symbolic of our industrial power, all the vegetation has withered away. Beside it the water runs a deep blue-green; not naturally, but from the chemicals which are poured into it along its course.

Yet smoke is the gauge of prosperity in the Valley. To the resident who points with pride at the smoking stacks, it means that his town is thriving; and the men are at work, that times are good.

47   *Weirton, West Virginia, home of the Great "Big Tin Can."*

46   *Pittsburgh Coke Company's works at Clairton, Pennsylvania.*

48 *Street adjoining the steel mills in Lorain, Ohio.*

49 *Automatic car wash near the steel mills in Lorain, Ohio.*

Pittsburgh, Pennsylvania, beneath the Bloomfield Bridge.

A RAGE UPON THE LAND

. . . just as it was the white man's way to assert himself in any landscape, to change it, make it over a little (at least to leave some mark of memorial of his sojourn), it was the Indian's way to pass through a country without disturbing anything; to pass and leave no trace, like fish through the water, or birds through the air.

It was the Indian manner to vanish into the landscape, not to stand out against it.

In the working of silver or drilling of turquoise the Indians had exhaustless patience; upon their blankets and belts and ceremonial robes they lavished their skill and pains. But their conception of decoration did not extend to the landscape. They seemed to have none of the European's desire to 'master' nature, to arrange and re-create. They spent their ingenuity in the other direction; in accommodating themselves to the scene in which they found themselves. This was not so much from indolence, . . . as from an inherited caution and respect. It was as if the great country were asleep, and they wished to carry on their lives without wakening it; or as if the spirits of earth and air and water were things not to antagonize and arouse. When they hunted, it was with the same discretion; an Indian hunt was never a slaughter. They ravaged neither the rivers nor the forest, and if they irrigated, they took as little water as would serve their needs. The land and all that it bore they treated with consideration; not attempting to improve it, they never desecrated it.

WILLA CATHER
Death Comes For The Archbishop

The prevailing winds on this continent are the Westerlies, and when they blow they bring the hope to those who must breathe the insidious poisons in the atmosphere that they will clear the air and cleanse the land.

Eminent Domain is perhaps the greatest threat to our property of any power of government. The Right of Eminent Domain is the sovereign power to condemn and take private property for public use with "just" compensation, such compensation being monetary only. And the right of compensation is the only constitutional protection we have; it is left to the courts to determine what is "just" and to interpret "public use."

The exercise of Eminent Domain implies that "we the people" shall benefit from it, that the principle of the greatest good for the greatest number shall be true always.

We justify the fact that for the Interstate Highway system alone we will have taken 750,000 pieces of property from our citizens, because they will benefit from the gift of greater mobility, the opportunity to travel anywhere and to enjoy the countryside; and perhaps because the National Guard tanks and busloads of police may roll more swiftly on their way to quell "disturbances."

Our rights to have and to hold property, to own a home, are indeed precarious so long as we are willing to exchange them for the right to go everywhere in our cars.

53   *Aiming at Chicago's heart, the Dan Ryan Expressway cuts a devastating swath northward, splitting the neighborhoods of the city's South Side. Its sixteen lanes are possibly unequalled in number by any other freeway in America, and have successfully dismembered the communities which lay in its path, forever, in order that the people who live some place else, can get some where else.*

        Today, looking like an afterthought, there are two tracks of rapid transit line down the median strip of this freeway. What is tragically absurd is that even one *track has the carrying capacity of* ten *lanes of road.*

52   *The view from the front porch of a house on a street dead-ended by Interstate 20 in Atlanta, Georgia.*

The pavement area of the [proposed Inter-
state] system assembled in one huge park-
ing lot . . . could accommodate two-thirds of
all the motor vehicles in the United States.
New right of way needed amounts to 1½
million acres. Total excavations will move
enough material to bury Connecticut knee
deep in dirt.

UNITED STATES BUREAU OF
PUBLIC ROADS

54 *Interstate 84 Expressway at Hartford, Connecticut,*
September 1966.

Not like the brazen giant of Greek fame,
With conquering limbs astride from land to land;
Here at our sea-washed, sunset gates shall stand
A mighty woman with a torch, whose flame
Is the imprisoned lightning, and her name
Mother of Exiles. From her beacon-hand
Glows world-wide welcome; her mild eyes command
The air-bridged harbor that twin cities frame.
"Keep, ancient lands, your storied pomp!" cries she
With silent lips. "Give me your tired, your poor,
Your huddled masses yearning to breathe free,
The wretched refuse of your teeming shore.
Send these, the homeless, tempest-tost to me,
I lift my lamp beside the golden door!"

*Sonnet by Emma Lazarus on a plaque at the base
of the Statue of Liberty.*

56 *"Pizza Town U.S.A.", on U.S. Highway 46 in New Jersey.*

57 *Driving range and miniature golf course on Route 17,*
near Ridgefield, New Jersey.

58 *Used car dealer's billboard in Union, New Jersey.*

The subjugation of the American Indian was complete long before 1907, when the last remnant of Indian Territory vanished with the admission of Oklahoma into the Union.

Because, simply by his presence on the land, the Indian stood in the way of the fulfillment of our "Manifest Destiny," he became the victim in a kind of Holy War resulting in the virtual destruction of his culture and nearly complete annihilation of his race. The history of this conflict has been glorified in our minds for generations. Perhaps it substantiated the belief that we as a nation know above all how to get things done efficiently, even if it means exterminating a race of people in the process.

Ironically, in the campaign against the red man our relentlessness became a virtue in our minds. The nation, fresh from "success" in the Civil War, had a ready-made military machine whose energy could be put to good use in solving the Indian problem once and for all so that we could get on with the business of settling our country. After the last battle, the ravaged tribes were for the most part rounded up and driven onto what are euphemistically called "reservations," but which in reality are hardly more than ghettos. There, in these red ghettos, forgotten because they are far away from us, "the first Americans" are being digested slowly by our culture, our religion, and our technology: the white man's way.

"Treat all men alike. Give them all the same law. Give them all an even chance to live and grow. All men were made by the same Great Spirit Chief. They are all brothers. The earth is the mother of all people, and all people should have equal rights upon it."

CHIEF JOSEPH, 1879

Indian reservation on the Cariboo Trail near Cache Creek, British Columbia.

NEGLECT AND SOLITUDE

Upon the American landscape today are strewn the castaways of our history. Neglected and decaying, they are the buildings and machines which, through no inherent defect in design or function, have ceased to be of use to us. Architecture, despite its seemingly indestructible nature, often turns out to be startlingly ephemeral: social changes and changes in style, economic changes, changes in priorities may determine the fate of a structure. It may be condemned for no other cause than that the land it occupies is needed for something else. Perhaps more than others, commercial and industrial buildings are vulnerable. Like the cans and bottles which are sown idly across the face of the nation, the shells of buildings which once contained some useful enterprise or served some vital function are discarded. Once the contents have been consumed, the container itself seems to have no further value.

What we keep and what we discard, in final analysis, is decided by the impersonal criterion of whether or not it is profitable to operate or economic to maintain. Once a thing becomes a liability to its owner, it is disposed of, unless it can be adapted easily to some other use. Often it is discarded, simply left for someone in another generation to dispose of. Thus, we have the powerful irony of man's destructive neglect of the very instruments of possession which he created to subdue the land.

The automobile has had perhaps a more profound effect than anything else on the fate of architecture and building in America, both in what it has created and in what it has destroyed. Osbert Lancaster has called the automobile "the most effective wrecker of beauty, both architectural and natural." In the process of rendering Main Street obsolete, it has created the great architectural wasteland of the roadside strip and suburbia. Downtown has given way to out-of-town shopping centers, resulting in communities with empty centers waiting for their urban renewal projects, and the false promise of a new life. The automobile is not only altering the very nature of our cities and countryside but is transforming our national character as well. In America, our cars have effectively abolished the hope of having a decent public land transportation system ever again, unless our attitudes and priorities are changed drastically. The passenger trains are gone, and when they stopped running the buildings that went with them, the depots, were shut up. In the shadows of bridges, erected by demand of impatient vehicle·owners, are the abandoned ferry houses and the rotting boats which once bound the communities on opposite banks together. Now these towns, cut off, stare like strangers at each other across the river, since to save money most bridges have no footpaths.

Though the effect of the automobile is catastrophic, it is not the sole illustration of how vulnerable what we make is to the social and economic pressures we ourselves promote. The creation of obsolescence is, in fact, the sustaining process of technology. According to economic laws nothing is inviolate; our towns, our houses, our factories, our monuments are equally expendable. Often because of differences of no more than a few pennies, both the market value and the competitive position of an enterprise have been ruined along with all the places depending on it for livelihood. The ghost town is not indigenous to the West. America has many regions filled with decaying communities. Take just one example from the dreary valleys of Appalachia— the anthracite country of Pennsylvania, where unfortunate thousands are condemned to sit idly on their stoops waiting for their relief checks, unable to find work and unable to escape. When natural and economic catastrophe combine, they can deal a devastating blow to entire regions, as the Dust Bowl showed. In many places, particularly near great metropolitan areas, the practice of farming has become obsolete because of a new priority for acreage caused by the pressures of swelling populations.

Our civilization is changing so rapidly that we cannot cope with its problems, much less with those created by the things we discard in our hurry to embrace something newer. There is no pressing reason to do anything about our rejects; the land is full of poignant structures representing facets of our history, not as monuments to the past, but as expressions of ourselves. They are like tombstones, but they symbolize, more than anything else, human travail. If these seemingly impervious buildings are so susceptible to change, what about us? What about the fragile, perishable quality of the human spirit, so vulnerable to indifference? Is it, too, only a commodity subject to economic laws? Is it to be castaway as well?

60 *Main Street of Faxon, population 137, on the fringes of the Red River Valley in southwestern Oklahoma.*

The "Dust Bowl," broadly speaking, is a term applicable to the Great Plains, especially the southwestern corner, but the term carries a more than geographical significance. Since the 1930s it has come to symbolize the disaster that always stalks the farmer. The tragic catastrophe which fell upon the Dust Bowl plains in the thirties was as much the fault of the farmer as of the weather. In our ignorance we plowed under the ancient grasslands, because being from the wet East we did not understand how to treat our arid Great Plains. We tried to bring this land under the same intensive cultivation that we had practiced at home. Instead of adapting to the land we tried to make it adapt to us; and we failed. We broke the sod, planted our crops, and when they began to fail, we prayed. But in spite of prayers there came upon the land in the mid-thirties a terrible drought. The crops withered away the first season; the next there were fewer to die. The soil thus exposed lay baking under the sun and as the winds dried it out it was carried away in great black clouds.

The nation was in the midst of a great Depression which caused thousands upon thousands of farmers to fail all across the land; in the Dust Bowl the combination of drought and depression was catastrophic.

The spectres of the Dust Bowl, the poverty-stricken farmer—Steinbeck's Joads, the people of Woody Guthrie's ballads—still haunt the plains, even today strewn with abandoned homesteads, their broken banging windmills standing alone on the quarter-sections where their owners once so passionately strove to bring forth the elusive bounty of the land.

On this land, too, are scores of nearly-dead towns, where there is invariably a post office, more than likely a brand-new one, beside the abandoned bank, and empty stores, which are all always there. The post office is there for the few people who still live on in the houses in the side streets; it is their address.

Upstate New York, like much of the Northeast, is traditionally dairy country. The rolling farmlands of Delaware, Dutchess, Orange, and Sullivan Counties, in the state's southern corner, were once New York City's milkshed from which it drew most of its supply. It came down the valleys on milk trains whose whistles echoed back and forth early in the morning. On its way, the train paused here and there at trackside creameries where the farmers had brought their produce, to pick up a car or two before whistling away again, filling the valley with sound.

Lordville, New York, is on the Erie's main line far up the Delaware River in this dairy country. On the tracks which pass by the town, countless freight trains roll through the valley without stopping. Yet steam engines once paused here to take water; there was a depot, where the mail came and went by passenger trains which stopped there momentarily. Even before this was a dairyland, it was a lumbering and tanning center with a siding or two, near which stood other trackside buildings where freight cars came to be loaded and unloaded. In those days the rails through Lordville shone brighter.

Trucks killed the milk trains long ago, and the little towns around the creameries began to dry up; they became mere clusters of houses, huddling around the crumbling remnants of former enterprises. Lordville, and hundreds of towns like it, has been bypassed; totally dependent upon the railroad for its life, it was severed from the outside world once the trains stopped stopping there.

The Northeast has never been kind to the farmer. It is rocky, hilly country, whose natural state is wooded. For generations men have sought to glean a living from hillside farms hewn from the forest. Some among them who farmed the richer bottom lands of the valleys or the fertile plains next to Lake Champlain or Maine's Aroostook County fared better. But for all farmers, the winters are cold, and the growing season short. It is a land of the small farm, not a land suited to the great farm factories of the West and South which need huge acreages to produce the big cash crops—wheat, and corn, and cotton —and where gigantic holdings allow a few farmers to get rich on government subsidies, while the Vermont farmer must be content with hay and his hard-earned milk checks.

But to the observer, it is a gentle land; one of unparalleled pastoral beauty in which man and nature seem to have achieved a balance. If a balance exists, perhaps it is because the small farmer has not been able to manipulate his environment but has adapted to it in order to survive. Because of the way the farmer has used it, the landscape has become the embodiment of "country." The relationship between man and the land, which created this beautiful countryside, is always fragile at best, and in the Northeast

it is especially so because real estate has become more profitable than farming. Lying near the great Eastern cities, this land is gobbled up in vast tracts by the cities' commerce, or, taken over piecemeal by the city-dweller seeking escape, each man grabbing his own little half-acre plot. And over the boulevards by the busload come the masses bound for their resorts. For them the land has no intrinsic value; they are drawn by the intangible qualities of physical beauty, of "peace" and "harmony." But the more playground replaces farmland, the more the beauty fades. The overgrown pastures are suitable only for housing developments, the remaining farmers readily sell out, for they have struggled too long. The process is at first imperceptible but becomes more obvious as it becomes irreversible.

The transitional state is cruelly tantalizing and the ugliest of all: the land is still filled with rural patches, the barns are still there, but there are no more cows, all the animals are gone, and around the next bend the fields are filling with the tacky vanguard of civilization. When, at last, the transformation is complete, when megalopolis has finally made over the whole scene, and we don't expect to find "country," perhaps then it will be easier to accept.

62 *Abandoned barn on the River Road, Putney, Vermont.*

63 *A farm on the bank of the sea, overlooking the Gulf of St. Lawrence near Cap Lumière, New Brunswick, where the sandy soil is as poor as the farmer who tries to eke a living from it.*

In March of 1959, the New York Central Railroad discontinued its ferry service on the Hudson River from Weehawken, New Jersey, to New York City, having convinced the powers who regulate commerce that the costs of operating it were incalculably high. The commuters still using the dwindling number of passenger trains were thus left stranded on the opposite shore, and soon thereafter they forsook the railroad altogether. With the line unused, of course, the railroad company soon proved without a doubt that the trains were unprofitable, and so was able to discontinue them as well, and close down the whole Weehawken Passenger Terminal. This monstrous wooden structure was built by the New York, West Shore & Buffalo Railroad in the 1880s, in anticipation of the crowds of Niagara-bound passengers it hoped to woo away from the New York Central which eventually was forced to buy it off. Throngs of vacationers filed through its halls each season, until the automobile began to siphon away the railroad's patrons, as more tunnels were bored and the river was bridged more frequently.

Eventually, only the commuters were left, though they were still a substantial group. The majority were whisked directly across the river to Forty-second Street, but those heading to Wall Street on the Cortlandt Street boat could start the day with the longest ferry ride in the harbor, a twenty-five minute steam down the river in the morning past midtown skyscrapers and great ocean liners berthed along the New York shore, and they could end it with another in the twilight on the way home. Today the same commuter, like most of his fellows from New Jersey, is sucked under the river in a filthy, gas-filled tube.

As is always the case with the abandonment of a service like a ferry or a train running on a fixed schedule familiar to all who use it, it seems that it is really not possible to comprehend what it will be like without it—until it is gone. Months after the last boat whistled off, there was still, in the door of the fruitstand in Weehawken, a sign hastily written by the proprietor: "Closed temporarily, will reopen soon."

But no one ever came to catch a ferry at Weehawken again. Early in the morning of August 21, 1961 the entire building burned to the ground.

64 *Ferry terminal at Weehawken, New Jersey.*

65   *The ferry boat,* Ellis Island, *has been rotting in its slip since 1954, when the government abandoned its immigration station on the island. Since 1892 Ellis Island had been the chief point of entry for over 16,000,000 immigrants who passed through its halls on their way to the promised land.*

For many of us living at a time when the American passenger train is in grave danger of extinction, it is almost impossible to realize how important it once was.

So widespread was the railroad's passenger service in its heyday, that virtually every settlement on a rail line had a depot wherein sat an agent of the company to serve its customers. To many a community the railroad station was the focus of all communication with the outside. The trains stopping there carried not only the people, but their goods, their baggage and their mail as well; they could carry a person as far beyond the horizons as the rails went and bring him home again. At the depot we sent our telegrams, and waited for the answers. More often, it was just a place to wait in anticipation of those scheduled moments when the rest of the country passed for an instant at 12:11 or 4:20 or 6:25; a man could feel a part of it all.

Usually the depot was a simple structure, albeit with unmistakable characteristics. There was often a standard design used by a line for smaller towns, and another, perhaps more imposing one, for the more important places. But they were built in every architectural style and combination of styles.

Today over ninety percent of us who travel from place to place use our own cars; the rest of us, exclusive of commuters, use airplanes or buses, and an ever-diminishing number use trains.

As train service is cut back more and more, so are the depot's functions, often purposely, as if to drive away the few patrons who are left just to prove that no one uses it any more. Most of our remaining passenger stations are in a sad state of partial decay and neglect. Like any piece of commercial property, they are taxable even when unused, so they are among the first targets of economy-conscious railroad managements. A few are sold for other uses— gas stations, stores, houses, even post offices —but more are simply torn down, often before the trains have stopped running.

The railroad station at North Easton, Massachusetts, is one of a very few depots built by a major American architect.

It is one of five buildings which H. H. Richardson put up during the 1880s, all commissioned by the Ames family, whose shovelworks were the town's principal industry. These buildings are not only a monument to Richardson, but are a rare exemplification of what an enlightened patron and a great architect could do for a company town.

Of the five buildings, only the railroad station has suffered badly and is now in a derelict state, having been damaged by fire and vandalism. Whether the responsibility for its maintenance belongs with the railroad, the town, or the Ames family is a continuing controversy. Commissioned in November 1881, it was served by the Old Colony Railroad which became part of the New Haven before being swallowed up by the Penn-Central. It has not seen passenger service for decades.

66 *Railroad station at North Easton, Massachusetts.*

The main line of the Central Railroad of
New Jersey from Jersey City to Scranton,
Pennsylvania, used to have one of the finest
groups of stations of any railroad in the
country. Where once trains with names
such as "The Queen of the Valley" and
"The Philadelphia Flyer" stopped, today
only dingy commuter trains serve the line's
stations in suburban New Jersey. Beyond
the range of the commuter, across the
Delaware and up the Lehigh Valley, it is
now "Freight Service Only."

67   *The Central Railroad of New Jersey's station*
in Fanwood, New Jersey.

Staircase in the Central Railroad of New Jersey's passenger station in Wilkes-Barre, Pennsylvania.

69   *Jim Thorpe, Pennsylvania, was formerly better known as Mauch Chunk to the throngs who detrained at the Lehigh Valley station on their way to the Poconos resorts. The Route of The Black Diamond discontinued passenger trains over a decade ago, and after years of abandonment this wonderful building was demolished and a supermarket built to take its place.*

70 *Scales by ticket window of one of great railroad stations in America, the Reading Company's Outer Station, in the railroad's home-town, Reading, Pennsylvania.*

71 *Flag and radiator in waiting room.*

73 *Northbound platform of Delaware & Hudson*
Railroad's station at Whitehall, New York.

As a nation we pride ourselves on our mobility; from the point of view of the mileage an average American travels in his lifetime, we outdistance any other people. On our own continent the main instrument of this mobility is the automobile, which we believe gives us the freedom, the potential ability, to go anywhere we want, whenever we want. We are freed from the shackles of public transportation. There, in our garage, or parked in front of our house, is an automobile, one of 87,000,000 in the nation. What is ironic about having a car is that while we believe it increases our ability to come in contact with the rest of the country, to touch different facets and people in the land, it is not actually so. We are imprisoned in our vehicles. Locked into our cars, we are actually more isolated on the highway than anywhere else. Confined by it, we are slave to it, and it is a slave to the highway. Rather than expanding our horizons, it is, in fact, an extension of our private domain, within which we are enclosed, insulated from the outside world as if in a chrysalis. We get into that familiar vehicle, settle into the contoured control seat behind the wheel, turn the key, rev up the engine, turn on the radio, air-conditioner, heater, whatever, and roll away onto the cement ribbon. Once on the road we can't see anything really for it all goes by too fast; the better the road, the quicker the countryside rushes past. We can't smell flowers, nor slow down fast enough to pick one, if we wanted to. We can see beautiful things, but they are always over the fence just out of reach, beyond the right-of-way; or it is just too much trouble to stop.

We have become a nation of "indolent millions, born on wheels and suckled on gasoline," spoiled because our nation is geared to the driver. There are drive-ins and -ups for every purpose; banks, churches, restaurants, telephones, mailboxes, even mortuaries! We are people who shoot deer from our cars. A car is a vehicle in which we entertain, a mobile boudoir. To make contact with anything outside our car becomes an effort, because we don't have to once we are in it. We pat ourselves on the back if we actually are able to emerge and take one step to look, *feel*, at a "scenic overlook." The people one meets: gas station attendants, motel keepers, waitresses, toll collectors, park rangers, are automatons, playing their roles. Why then, have we sacrificed our precious land, if we can go no further than ourselves?

It is surprising how dependent we are upon the illusion that owning a car makes us *free*, though in the end it may mean sacrificing everything, giving up the land we cherish and want to enjoy. We build more roads to get to every remote, beautiful place so that we can see it, forgetting that in doing so we destroy it forever. This is the great sorrow of the automobile age. But the exquisite irony is one recognized by pragmatists, that even though the magic qualities of the automobile are illusory, we would have a national catastrophe if we stopped producing cars at an ever-increasing rate. The automobile is a necessity to our economy, it has become almost un-American *not* to own one, and in a personal sense we believe it is a necessity, too, not a luxury, but a Right.

74　*Car heading north on Interstate 91*
along the side of Lamentation Mountain,
near Berlin, Connecticut.

A species once extinguished is never
repeated. November 22, 1967—the *Elmira*
crosses the river for the last time. Fly-
ing a jack as is the custom to mark the
final day or voyage in the life of a vessel, she signals the end of ferryboating on
the Hudson. In her slow progress, as if
passing over the Styx, she is a frighten-
ing augury of man's own fate.

REFERENCES

Andrews, Wayne, editor. *Concise Dictionary of American History*. New York: Charles Scribner's Sons, 1962.

Bailey, Thomas A. *The American Pageant*. Boston: D. C. Heath and Company, 1956.

Cather, Willa. *Death Comes for the Archbishop.* Borzoi Books. New York: Alfred A. Knopf, Inc., 1951.

Downing, Andrew Jackson. *A Treatise on the Theory of Landscape Gardening*. New York: Wiley and Putnam, 1841.

————. *Cottage Residences*. New York: Wiley and Putnam, 1842.

Gropius, Walter, "Die Kunst in Industrie und Handel," *Jahrbuch des Deutschen Werkbundes*, Jena, 1913, as quoted in Siegfried Giedion. *Space, Time and Architecture*. Cambridge: Harvard University Press, 1959.

Harte, Francis Bret. *Poems*. Boston: James R. Osgood and Company, 1875.

Le Corbusier. *Towards A New Architecture*. Translated by Frederick Etchells. New York: Payson and Clarke Ltd., 1927.

Mowbray, A. Q. *Road to Ruin*. Philadelphia: J. B. Lippincott Company, 1969.

O'Sullivan, John L. "Editorial," *Democratic Review*, July-August 1845.

Ruskin, John. *The Seven Lamps of Architecture*. London: Smith, Elder and Company, 1849.